THE
SOUTH
AMERICANS

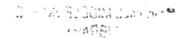

THE SOUTH AMERICANS

Alan Cullison

CHELSEA HOUSE PUBLISHERS

New York   Philadelphia

On the cover: South American members of the Spanish choir at Our Lady of Fatima Church in Jackson Heights, New York.

CHELSEA HOUSE PUBLISHERS

Editor-in-Chief: Remmel Nunn
Managing Editor: Karyn Gullen Browne
Copy Chief: Juliann Barbato
Picture Editor: Adrian G. Allen
Art Director: Maria Epes
Deputy Copy Chief: Mark Rifkin
Assistant Art Director: Loraine Machlin
Manufacturing Manager: Gerald Levine
Systems Manager: Lindsey Ottman
Production Manager: Joseph Romano
Production Coordinator: Marie Claire Cebrián

The Peoples of North America

Senior Editor: Kathy Kuhtz

Staff for THE SOUTH AMERICANS

Assistant Editor: Scott Prentzas
Copy Editor: Joseph Roman
Picture Research: Wendy P. Wills
Senior Designer: Noreen Romano
Cover Illustration: Paul Biniasz
Banner Design: Hrana Janto

3   5   7   9   8   6   4

Library of Congress Cataloging-in-Publication Data
Cullison, Alan.
  The South Americans/Alan Cullison.
    p.—cm.—(The Peoples of North America)
  Includes bibliographical references.
  Summary: Discusses the history, culture, and religion of the South Americans, their place in American society, and the problems they face as an ethnic group in North America.
  1. Hispanic Americans—Juvenile literature. [1. Hispanic Americans.] I. Title. II. Series.
E184.S75C85 1990
973'.0468—dc20   90-1412
ISBN 0-87754-863-3   CIP
    0-7910-0305-1 (pbk.)   AC

CONTENTS

THE PEOPLES OF NORTH AMERICA

CHELSEA HOUSE PUBLISHERS

A NATION
OF NATIONS

Daniel Patrick Moynihan

The Constitution of the United States begins: "We the People of the United States . . . " Yet, as we know, the United States is not made up of a single group of people. It is made up of many peoples. Immigrants from Europe, Asia, Africa, and Central and South America settled in North America seeking a new life filled with opportunities unavailable in their homeland. Coming from many nations, they forged one nation and made it their own. More than 100 years ago, Walt Whitman expressed this perception of America as a melting pot: "Here is not merely a nation, but a teeming Nation of nations."

Although the ingenuity and acts of courage of these immigrants, our ancestors, shaped the North American way of life, we sometimes take their contributions for granted. This fine series, *The Peoples of North America*, examines the experiences and contributions of the immigrants and how these contributions determined the future of the United States and Canada.

Immigrants did not abandon their ethnic traditions when they reached the shores of North America. Each ethnic group had its own customs and traditions, and each brought different experiences, accomplishments, skills, values, styles of dress, and tastes in food that lingered long after its arrival. Yet this profusion of differences created a singularity, or bond, among the immigrants.

The United States and Canada are unusual in this respect. Whereas religious and ethnic differences have sparked intolerance throughout the rest of the world—from the 17th-century religious wars to the 19th-century nationalist movements in Europe to the near extermination of the Jewish people under Nazi Germany—North Americans have struggled to learn how to respect each other's differences and live in harmony.

Millions of immigrants from scores of homelands brought diversity to our continent. In a mass migration, some 12 million immigrants passed through the waiting rooms of New York's Ellis Island; thousands more came to the West Coast. At first, these immigrants were welcomed because labor was needed to meet the demands of the Industrial Age. Soon, however, the new immigrants faced the prejudice of earlier immigrants who saw them as a burden on the economy. Legislation was passed to limit immigration. The Chinese Exclusion Act of 1882 was among the first laws closing the doors to the promise of America. The Japanese were also effectively excluded by this law. In 1924, Congress set immigration quotas on a country-by-country basis.

Such prejudices might have triggered war, as they did in Europe, but North Americans chose negotiation and compromise instead. This determination to resolve differences peacefully has been the hallmark of the peoples of North America.

The remarkable ability of Americans to live together as one people was seriously threatened by the issue of slavery. It was a symptom of growing intolerance in the world. Thousands of settlers from the British Isles had arrived in the colonies as indentured servants, agreeing to work for a specified number of years on farms or as apprentices in return for passage to America and room and board. When the first Africans arrived in the then-British colonies during the 17th century, some colonists thought that they too should be treated as indentured servants. Eventually, the question of whether the Africans should be viewed as indentured, like the English, or as slaves who could be owned for life, was considered in a Maryland court. The court's calamitous decree held that blacks were slaves bound to lifelong servitude, and so were their children. America went through a time of moral examination and civil war before it finally freed African slaves and their descendants. The principle that all people are created equal had faced its greatest challenge and survived.

Yet the court ruling that set blacks apart from other races fanned flames of discrimination that burned long after slavery was abolished—and that still flicker today. The concept of racism had existed for centuries in countries throughout the world. For instance, when the Manchus conquered China in the 13th century, they decreed that Chinese and Manchus could not intermarry. To impress their superiority on the conquered Chinese, the Manchus ordered all Chinese men to wear their hair in a long braid called a queue.

By the 19th century, some intellectuals took up the banner of racism, citing Charles Darwin. Darwin's scientific studies hypothesized that highly evolved animals were dominant over other animals. Some advocates of this theory applied it to humans, asserting that certain races were more highly evolved than others and thus were superior.

This philosophy served as the basis for a new form of discrimination, not only against nonwhite people but also against various ethnic groups. Asians faced harsh discrimination and were depicted by popular 19th-century newspaper cartoonists as depraved, degenerate, and deficient in intelligence. When the Irish flooded American cities to escape the famine in Ireland, the cartoonists caricatured the typical "Paddy" (a common term for Irish immigrants) as an apelike creature with jutting jaw and sloping forehead.

By the 20th century, racism and ethnic prejudice had given rise to virulent theories of a Northern European master race. When Adolf Hitler came to power in Germany in 1933, he popularized the notion of Aryan supremacy. *Aryan*, a term referring to the Indo-European races, was applied to so-called superior physical characteristics such as blond hair, blue eyes, and delicate facial features. Anyone with darker and heavier features was considered inferior.

Buttressed by these theories, the German Nazi state from 1933 to 1945 set out to destroy European Jews, along with Poles, Russians, and other groups considered inferior. It nearly succeeded. Millions of these people were exterminated.

The tragedies brought on by ethnic and racial intolerance throughout the world demonstrate the importance of North America's efforts to create a society free of prejudice and inequality.

A relatively recent example of the New World's desire to resolve ethnic friction nonviolently is the solution the Canadians found to a conflict between two ethnic groups. A long-standing dispute as to whether Canadian culture was properly English or French resurfaced in the mid-1960s, dividing the peoples of the French-speaking Quebec Province from those of the English-speaking provinces. Relations grew tense, then bitter, then violent. The Royal Commission on Bilingualism and Biculturalism was established to study the growing crisis and to propose measures to ease the tensions. As a result of the commission's recommendations, all official documents and statements from the national government's capital at Ottawa are now issued in both French and English, and bilingual education is encouraged.

The year 1980 marked a coming of age for the United States's ethnic heritage. For the first time, the U.S. Census asked people about their ethnic background. Americans chose from more than 100 groups, including French Basque, Spanish Basque, French Canadian, Afro-American, Peruvian, Armenian, Chinese, and Japanese. The ethnic group with the largest response was English (49.6 million). More than 100 million Americans claimed ancestors from the British Isles, which includes England, Ireland, Wales, and Scotland. There were almost as many Germans (49.2 million) as English. The Irish-American population (40.2 million) was third, but the next largest ethnic group, the Afro-Americans, was a distant fourth (21 million). There was a sizable group of French ancestry (13 million), as well as of Italian (12 million). Poles, Dutch, Swedes, Norwegians, and Russians followed. These groups, and other smaller ones, represent the wondrous profusion of ethnic influences in North America.

Canada, too, has learned more about the diversity of its population. Studies conducted during the French/English conflict showed that Canadians were descended from Ukrainians, Germans, Italians, Chinese, Japanese, native Indians, and Eskimos, among others. Canada found it had no ethnic majority, although nearly half of its immigrant population had come from the British Isles. Canada, like the United States, is a land of immigrants for whom mutual tolerance is a matter of reason as well as principle.

The people of North America are the descendants of one of the greatest migrations in history. And that migration is not over. Koreans, Vietnamese, Nicaraguans, Cubans, and many others are heading for the shores of North America in large numbers. This mix of cultures shapes every aspect of our lives. To understand ourselves, we must know something about our diverse ethnic ancestry. Nothing so defines the North American nations as the motto on the Great Seal of the United States: *E Pluribus Unum*—Out of Many, One.

TO SEEK A BETTER LIFE

The U.S. will do anything for Latin America except read about it," said James Reston, a political commentator, about the region. Only recently have North Americans begun to prove him wrong. Perhaps one reason for this is that Hispanics—a group that includes the Spanish- and Portuguese-speaking peoples of Central and South America, Mexico, and parts of the West Indies—are now one of the fastest-growing ethnic groups in North America. In the United States alone, the Hispanic population increased from 9 million (or 4.5 percent of the population) in 1970 to 25 million (or 10 percent of the population) in 1990. The vibrancy of Latin American culture and art, as well as the extreme wealth and poverty these newcomers have brought with them, has attracted much attention from politicians, scholars, and the news media in recent years.

This book is about South Americans who have migrated to the United States and Canada. South Americans have come to North America for the same reasons that have compelled millions of other immigrants to move to the continent: personal liberty and economic opportunity. Although South Americans are a relatively new and quite small immigrant group, they are one of the fastest-growing groups among Latin American immigrants and have begun to play a larger role in North American society as they arrive in ever-increasing numbers.

The first real wave of South American immigrants came to North America in the early 19th century. They settled in what is now the state of California, which was a province of Mexico until 1848. Peruvians, Chileans, and Argentines were among the Spanish-speaking majority that lived in Alta California (as the Mexicans called the region). Most of the South American families were headed by skilled workers, such as bakers and bricklayers. They were vastly outnumbered by the Sonorans of northwestern Mexico, who were generally poorer than the South Americans. The Spanish-speaking communities that existed in California in the mid-19th century were overwhelmed by the huge migration of English-speaking Americans and European immigrants who went west during the gold rush. From 1848 to 1850, the white population of California more than tripled.

After this period, South Americans tended to migrate to the larger cities throughout the United States and Canada. By the early 20th century, when more than 1 million immigrants entered the United States each year, only about 4,000 South Americans immigrated there annually. Political violence, such as that experienced in Colombia from 1948 to 1957, and severe economic collapses, such as the one in Peru in 1975, have sporadically compelled large waves of South American immigrants to come to North America. By 1970, first- and second-generation South Americans numbered more than

350,000, still a small number when compared to most other immigrant groups.

South Americans have become part of the new pattern of immigration in North America, which some have called the first great wave of non-European immigration. Beginning in the 1960s and continuing into the 1990s, the majority of immigrants who have journeyed to the United States and Canada did not emanate from Europe, as in the first half of the 20th century, but came instead from the Western Hemisphere—particularly Mexico, Cuba, and Central and South America—or from Asia—particularly Vietnam, China, Korea, and the Philippines. In the United States, Europeans accounted for only 12 percent of immigrants by the end of the 1980s.

Colombians and Ecuadorans are the largest South American immigrant groups living in the United States, but their numbers are difficult to estimate because many either do not stay for long or are in the country illegally. Today there are thousands of descendants of South Americans in the United States and Canada, some of whom have no doubt forgotten their ancestry and have lost their ties to the South American community. Large populations of South Americans live in the northeastern United States and in such major cities as Chicago, Los Angeles, Miami, and Toronto.

Because many South Americans who migrate to North America are well educated and come from a middle-class background, they tend to have better employment skills than members of other Latin American immigrant groups, such as the Mexicans and Central Americans. Despite such distinctions, North Americans often mistakenly categorize South Americans and other Hispanics as one people. Frequently, North Americans assume that they are listening to Mexicans or Puerto Ricans when they hear a street conversation in Spanish, but this is not always the case.

Similar to other Latin American groups, the vast majority of South American immigrants are Roman

A group of Argentine Americans wearing traditional costumes celebrate their heritage during a parade in New York City.

Catholic, speak Spanish, and identify with a Spanish or Portuguese cultural tradition. The countries of South America differ greatly, and emigrants take these differences with them when they move to North America. Those who come to the United States and Canada often settle in the same cities but live in different neighborhoods. For example, Brazilians speak Portuguese, not Spanish, and thus they share little common ground with other South Americans. And even those South Americans who do speak Spanish are driven apart by different histories and national loyalties. Colombians and Venezuelans, for instance, are usually intensely competitive with each other. And many Colombians are anxious to assure their neighbors that they are not Puerto Ricans. That many of the people from these two regions speak the same language does not necessarily unite them. In fact, when asked, many South Americans say that they speak Uruguayan or Ecuadoran, rather than Spanish. In cities such as New York, there are Colombian and Ecuadoran sections that are close to, but distinct from, other Latin American sections.

Nobody knows exactly how many South Americans have decided to move to the United States and Canada to find refuge in a stable economic and political system. Nor is it known whether these people will one day pack their bags and return to their home if the economic and political crises in Latin America subside. But whatever their goals of personal betterment, the influx of South Americans is a reminder that North America remains, to many, the promised land.

A woodcut depicts Spanish conquistador Francisco Pizarro capturing Atahualpa, the ruler of the Incan Empire, in 1533. After killing Atahualpa and easily defeating the Incan army, Pizarro's troops carried off a large quantity of gold as booty.

THE OTHER HALF OF THE NEW WORLD

The South American continent was first discovered by Europeans in 1498 when Christopher Columbus sailed into the Gulf of Paria in present-day Venezuela on his third voyage to the Western Hemisphere. Columbus, whose expeditions were supported by King Ferdinand V and Queen Isabella of Spain, had earlier stumbled upon the New World on his first voyage in 1492 while searching for a more direct trade route between Europe and southern Asia. Consequently, many continue to call the native peoples of the Americas "Indians," perpetuating Columbus's mistaken belief that he had landed on the Spice Islands near modern-day India. Columbus had, in fact, landed on San Salvador, an island located 250 miles northeast of Cuba.

The continent of South America is vast. It is nearly twice the size of the United States but is populated by only about 15 percent more people. Almost half of South America is wilderness made up of the rugged

Andes mountains, the densely vegetated tropical rain forests of Brazil and Bolivia, the windswept Atacama Desert of Chile, and the open plains of Argentina and Paraguay. It is connected to Central and North America by the tiny isthmus extending north from Colombia through Panama. Most of the continent's large cities are near its coasts.

South America is divided into 12 countries and French Guiana, an overseas department (province) of France. The nations vary greatly in geography, language, and historical and economic development. Brazil, the continent's largest country, occupies nearly half of South America and has a population of more than 150 million. More than 80 percent of Brazilians are dark-skinned mulattoes (people of mixed Caucasian and African ancestry), *mamelucos* (the Portuguese term for mestizos, people of mixed European and Indian ancestry), or pure African in origin. Large parts of Brazil are unsettled and unexplored. For example, the Amazon Basin in the northern part of the country is covered with swamps and thick forests that settlers have only recently begun to penetrate. On the other hand, Uruguay is one-fiftieth the size of Brazil and is more developed. It has only 3 million inhabitants, 95 percent of whom are Creoles (people of European descent born in the Western Hemisphere).

Colonial Foundations

South America remains a region with complex problems because of the legacy of its settlement. When Spanish and Portuguese expeditions first landed on the shores of the continent at the end of the 15th century, they encountered various tribes living along the shores of the Caribbean Sea and in the tropical rain forests. They also confronted three major native groups—the Chibcha, the Inca, and the Araucanians—that had settled near the Andes mountains. Scientists have different

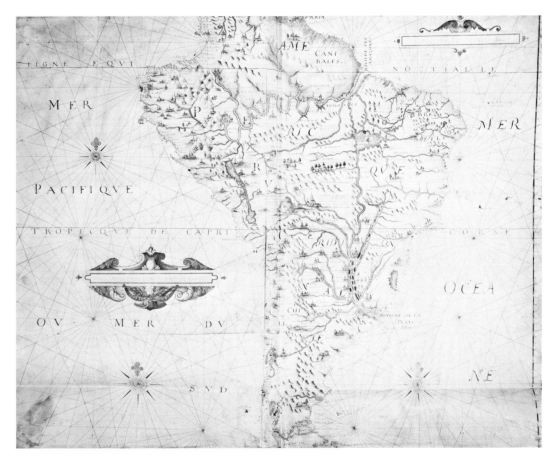

theories on how the ancestors of the original inhabitants of South America reached the continent. The most popular one is that they walked to the Western Hemisphere across a land bridge where the Bering Strait now separates North America and Asia. By about 6000 B.C., wandering tribes had settled as far as the southern tip of present-day Chile.

For thousands of years, the inhabitants of South America lived in small hunting groups, following herds of animals for food. Some tribes, particularly in the Andes, began to settle in permanent villages where they cultivated food, such as peanuts, cacaos, beans, corn,

A 17th-century map shows South America during its colonial period. Spanish and Portuguese forces had conquered and subjugated the native population by the mid-16th century, and settlers from the two countries soon established mines and plantations on the continent.

and tomatoes. As the populations increased, the villages grew into towns, cities, and entire civilizations.

When the Europeans arrived in the early 16th century, the Inca had established the largest and most advanced civilization in the Americas. Their empire controlled much of what is now Ecuador, Bolivia, and Peru and parts of Chile and Argentina. The Inca were expert builders and architects and constructed an extensive system of roads to connect their cities. Incan farmers carved elaborate terraces into mountainsides and built irrigation canals to provide water for their crops.

The Incan Empire, like other civilizations in the Western Hemisphere, was doomed by the arrival of European expeditions. Spain and Portugal began dividing the continent soon after they arrived in the late 15th century. Spain initially claimed all lands in South America 290 miles west of the Cape Verde Islands, but in 1494 the 2 European powers signed the Treaty of Tordesillas, which shifted the line of demarcation 1,100 miles farther west, giving Portugal the territory of modern-day Brazil and Spain the rest of the continent. The conquest of the Indians throughout South America came soon thereafter.

By the mid-16th century small groups of Spanish adventurers, mostly men who aspired to nobility and who called themselves conquistadores (conquerors), had vanquished all the major Indian civilizations in the New World. Most notably, in 1531 a small army led by Francisco Pizarro sailed from Panama to what is now Peru. They toppled the huge Incan Empire with relative ease by deceiving and murdering Atahualpa, the Incan king, and by defeating a large Incan army that had never before encountered guns or horses. Pizarro's army carted off as booty a hoard of gold that was large enough to fill a 12-by-17-foot room to the height of a man's waist.

As news of the riches of the New World filtered back to Spain and Portugal, more fortune seekers rushed to exploit the riches of the continent. The migration began even before the Spanish and Portuguese finished conquering the native populations. Many Europeans came in search of adventure and to find gold. Others, especially the Portuguese, established large plantations to grow such crops as sugarcane and tobacco to send back to Europe. In some areas, such as Argentina, the existing tribes were either killed off or driven away, leaving only the Europeans and African slaves, who were brought to South America to work on the plantations.

The ruins of Machu Picchu, an ancient Incan city built on a mountain in the Peruvian Andes, are a reminder of the great Incan Empire that ruled much of northwest South America from the 14th century until 1532. Machu Picchu was never found by the invading Spanish armies.

Nobody is sure about how many Indians lived on the continent when the Europeans arrived, but it is certain that the discovery and exploitation of the New World meant a slow death and a complete destruction of their way of life. During the early 16th century, Spain established the *encomienda* system, in which settlers were given large tracts of land, complete with the Indians who lived on them. The colonists collected tribute from the Indians for allowing them to live on the land that they once owned, and often they collected this tribute by forcing them to work on the land or in dark mines beneath it. In return, the colonists were supposed to protect the Indians from cruelty and convert them to Christianity. But millions of Indians died on the plantations and in the mines because of harsh treatment and overwork. Smallpox, a contagious disease brought to the New World by the Europeans, destroyed much of the Indian population, which lacked a natural immunity to the smallpox virus.

Between 1570 (40 years after the conquest) and 1620, the population of Indians in South America fell from about 1.3 million to about 600,000, a drop of more than 50 percent. As the population dwindled, European settlers, particularly those who owned sugar and coffee plantations, began importing slaves from Africa to replace the natives who were dying off. The native populations in northern Colombia and Brazil—two areas that had labor-intensive plantation economies—succumbed quickly, and many African slaves were brought into those areas. Large black populations live in Colombia and Brazil today.

In 1544, the Spanish established the viceroyalty of Peru, which encompassed all of the Spanish territories in South America until two additional viceroyalties (New Granada and La Plata) were established in the 18th century. In 1549, Portugal appointed a governor-general to administer its colony in Brazil. As colonial society in South America gradually established itself, so did the three power groups that ruled it. At the top were the government officials appointed by the Spanish and Portuguese rulers. The officials in each colony were not born in the New World but were Europeans. They controlled a highly centralized government in which only a few people held power, enabling the governments in Europe to control the colonies for one main purpose—to extract the continent's natural resources to the fullest.

The Roman Catholic clergy, another group in the ruling hierarchy, was responsible for educating the colonists and converting the slaves and Indians to Christianity. Roman Catholic missionaries had come to South America along with the Spanish and Portuguese excursions to save the souls of the conquered and, in their eyes, godless people of the continent. The missionaries, mostly from the Franciscan, Augustinian, Dominican, and Jesuit orders, established missions and schools throughout South America.

The third group wielding power in the New World were the landowners and the mine operators. In the early days of the colonial period, these people were native Europeans, but gradually they began to interbreed with the Indians, forming a group of people called mestizos. Mestizos make up the vast majority of South Americans today. Many European settlers chose to settle near the rich farmland or productive mines of the continent, far from the center of colonial government. As a consequence, many of them became the true arbiters of power in the regions where they lived. They no longer listened to the Spanish or Portuguese government for direction. Ultimately, it was this group that asserted itself and helped fight for independence from European rulers.

The Movement for Independence

Colonial rule in South America continued for more than 300 years. During that time, resentment toward European rule gradually grew, especially among the

Simón Bolívar, known as the Liberator, led the revolution against Spanish authority in northern South America. Like revolutionary leaders in the United States, Bolívar was influenced by the ideas of the Enlightenment, particularly the writings of French philosopher Jean-Jacques Rousseau. Bolívar dreamed of uniting South America into one great nation, but his goal was not achieved because control over the newly independent nations was soon seized by various dictators.

mestizos and Creoles. Many of the people who had settled in South America had amassed great wealth and property but were not allowed to assume a meaningful role in colonial government because they were not born in Europe. Colonists, especially the mestizos, were looked down upon by the Europeans and given very little opportunity to share in the power on the continent. Although Spain and Portugal introduced reforms allowing greater power to the colonists before 1800, the sentiment for revolution grew until it broke loose violently throughout South America early in the 19th century.

The great heroes in the fight for independence from Spanish rule in Latin America were Venezuelan general Simón Bolívar and Argentine general José de San Martín. Bolívar led armies through the continent that helped win independence for present-day Bolivia, Peru, Colombia, Ecuador, and Venezuela. San Martín helped fight for the independence of present-day Argentina,

General José de San Martín leads his regiment against Spanish forces in Peru. San Martín, who was born in present-day Argentina and educated in Spain, became a hero in South America for his military leadership in ousting the Spanish from Argentina, Chile, and Peru.

Chile, and Peru. Under the leadership of San Martín, landowners in Chile and Argentina won their independence by 1818 and later assisted in the fight for independence in the northern part of the continent. Bolívar and San Martín joined forces to oust the remaining Spanish troops from South America. Complete independence for the continent was assured in 1824 by the climactic defeat of Spanish forces at Ayacucho, Peru, at the hands of Antonio José de Sucre, Bolívar's foremost commander.

Pedro I, the son of King John VI of Portugal, declared Brazil's independence from Portugal in 1822 and became the first emperor of Brazil (1822–31).

Brazil, which had largely been settled by the Portuguese, managed to win its independence without violent revolution. The colonists saw their opportunity when Napoléon invaded Portugal in 1807 and the Portuguese ruler, Prince John, fled to Brazil. As Napoléon's power dwindled, John returned to Portugal 14 years later, leaving his son Pedro to rule the country. Ideas of revolution and independence had taken hold throughout South America, and many Brazilians expressed their dissatisfaction with European rule. Popular pressure compelled Pedro, who favored independence, to declare Brazil an independent empire in 1822, making himself Emperor Pedro I.

From Independence to Conflict

Today Bolívar is honored throughout South America as a savior because his leadership during the revolutions resulted in freedom from European rule. But independence brought problems to the continent that revolutionaries such as Bolívar, who died in 1830, could never resolve. During the colonial period, South Americans were governed by distant monarchs and had little voice in their own affairs. As a consequence, those who rebelled and established their own country had little experience in government. Many military leaders of the revolutionary forces were ambitious men who seized power in a number of countries. Thus, the independence movements often led to the establishment of new dictatorships that were headed by continental despots rather than European ones.

One disappointment to the revolutionaries was that independence did not bring unity to the continent. As soon as the various independent countries of the continent had been established, they began disputing their borders. In 1825, war broke out between Brazil and Argentina over territory bordering both countries that had been annexed by Brazil. A treaty signed three years later established this disputed territory as the country

of Uruguay, which was intended to act as a buffer between the two nations. In the War of the Triple Alliance (1865–75), about half of Paraguay's population was wiped out when Argentina, Brazil, and Uruguay attacked it in a border dispute. In the War of the Pacific (1879–83), Chile fought Peru and Bolivia for control over the large, nitrate-rich areas along the Pacific Ocean. Chile won the war and seized the area, leaving Bolivia landlocked. From 1932 to 1935, Bolivia and Paraguay

Bolivian troops use artillery against Paraguayan fortifications during the Chaco War (1932–35). Paraguay prevailed in the war and captured most of the Chaco, the plains located west of the Paraguay River that were being disputed by the two countries.

fought over the Chaco, a lowland area bordering the two countries. Most of the area was eventually ceded to Paraguay. Peru and Ecuador have fought several times during the early 20th century over an uncharted, mostly unexplored area in the Amazon River Basin between Ecuador and Brazil. Peru annexed the area in the 1940s, but Ecuador still claims it. Another continuing dispute is the one between Venezuela and Guyana; Venezuela claims about two-thirds of that country.

Another problem with the independence movements was that they did not bring any real change to the majority of people in South America. Slavery throughout Latin America was abolished by the late 19th century, but inequalities between light-skinned and darker-skinned South Americans remained. After the independence movements, all Indians were declared legal citizens, but the social conditions of Indians, poor mestizos, and blacks remained unchanged. And, if anything, they worsened. Indian peasants were conscripted to fight for causes that they did not understand. They were obliged to pay taxes to a central government run by city folk who were often not sympathetic to, or even aware of, peasant problems and beliefs.

Neither South America's independence movements nor many of the subsequent revolutionary movements that have swept the continent periodically have altered the social situation. Those who are in charge of the governments now tend to be white South Americans instead of white Europeans who ruled during the colonial period. In Ecuador, for example, the overwhelming majority of nonwhites and poor people are uneducated and detached from the mainstream of society. According to a study conducted by the University of Ecuador, for instance, 70 percent of the highland Indians of that country cannot name the country's president or the colors of its flag. They understandably find economic opportunities scant on a continent where in some places the popular word for Indian remains *chancho* ("pig").

Economic and Political Problems

South American countries have sought prosperity by producing one or two major commodities for overseas markets. Historically, Venezuela has relied on oil exports, Colombia on coffee, Chile on copper, and Bolivia on tin. This reliance on a single export has left the economies of many South American nations extremely susceptible to fluctuations in the world market for the particular product. For example, the economic depressions of some South American countries during the 1980s were as severe as the one that hit the United States in the 1930s.

Since 1900, the export-oriented economies have brought periods of remarkable prosperity to some countries. For example, Argentina became so wealthy from its export of beef and wheat that its capital, Buenos

A rancher and his gauchos (cowboys of the South American pampa) herd cattle in Argentina. Beef products have been Argentina's chief export for many years. The dependence of South American economies on a few products have made them susceptible to declines in the worldwide prices of those goods.

Aires, established itself as the "Paris of the South." By the 1920s, it was a large and cosmopolitan city of more than 750,000. Chile acquired similar wealth with its copper exports and some fruits and wheat that it produced for the international market.

However, there have been serious setbacks. The worldwide depression of the 1930s was a strain on the young industrial economies of South America. Millions were thrown out of work in cities from Colombia to Chile. Both the demand for and the value of products that the countries exported declined drastically as Europeans and residents of the United States stopped buying goods. Money that South American countries earned from exports shrank by about one-half from 1930 to 1934, putting extreme pressure on the governments there. Within a year of the stock market crash in the United States in 1929, army officers had sought or taken power by force in Brazil, Chile, Peru, and Argentina.

After the depression, many South American countries tried to revive their economies by exporting goods once again and diversifying the products that they produced. Until recently, most succeeded fairly well. Financed by foreign banks, many South American economies grew rapidly for more than a generation before 1981. From 1960 to 1980, most of the countries had a growth rate double that of the United States, although rising unemployment in many of them remained a problem.

But Chile, Brazil, Venezuela, and Argentina—the continent's most populous countries—have had difficulties because their income still depends largely on the whims of world markets that are sometimes thriving and at other times depressed. The price of some of the important export goods of South American countries—wheat, oil, coffee, and copper—have been at times worth only about as much as they were during the depression.

During the periodic economic hardships, military regimes have often taken control of the governments, ostensibly to repair the struggling economies and to jail members of purported pro-Communist organizations that identified themselves with the struggle against poverty and class distinctions. Military takeovers have occurred in most of the major countries of South America at one time or another: Brazil beginning in 1964; Uruguay in June 1973; Chile in September 1973; and Argentina in 1976. Political and economic refugees have streamed from one country to the next; and during the 1960s, when many Latin American countries ran into severe economic trouble again, the first large-scale immigration of South Americans to North America began.

Soldiers round up curfew violators in Valparaíso, Chile, in November 1973. Violent military takeovers, such as the one that ousted President Salvador Allende in Chile, have rocked several South American countries throughout the 20th century, compelling many people to seek refuge abroad.

A woman and her children stand in front of their home in a Lima, Peru, ghetto in April 1985. She has posted a placard supporting presidential candidate Alfonso Barrantes, an "advocate of the poor." The standard of living for most South Americans plunged in the 1980s, causing an increase in poverty and political unrest.

South America's debt crisis and ailing economies during the 1980s have caused many to write off this period as a lost decade because the standard of living for most South Americans declined to the levels experienced in the 1950s. In 1988, Brazil suffered inflation of more than 900 percent. Government officials in Peru, where the crisis was most dramatic, estimate that about 100,000 of its citizens fled to other countries to escape the economic tailspin in 1988. During 1988, inflation exceeded 1,900 percent in Peru, and real wages fell by more than half. In the spring of 1989, Venezuela, one of the continent's most stable democracies, suspended many constitutional rights for the first time since 1960 because the price of oil, its main export, had declined radically, causing economic hardships that led to rioting.

A woman removes broken panes from the windows of her apartment in Bogotá, Colombia, after a bomb destroyed a travel agency on the ground floor of the building. Many middle-class South Americans have migrated to North America to escape the escalating political and, in the case of Colombia, drug-related violence in their homeland.

LEAVING HOME

The earliest South American immigrants began leaving their homelands for North America in the early 19th century. By the early 20th century, when an average of 1 million people immigrated to the United States each year, approximately 4,000 South Americans came to the United States annually. South Americans did not arrive in large enough numbers to establish strong communities until after World War II. It was then that commercial air travel became more widely available to many middle-class South Americans. By 1970, first- and second-generation South Americans numbered more than 350,000 in the United States, and by 1980 the number had increased to an estimated 500,000. The precise number of South Americans in the United States and Canada is difficult to determine because many are in the countries illegally, either by overstaying their visits on tourist or student visas or by sneaking across the U.S. border by way of Mexico.

A slum area sits on a hillside on the outskirts of Cali, Colombia. Many of South America's larger cities have experienced overcrowding because of a high birthrate and the arrival of rural people in search of work. The number of jobs has not increased as rapidly as the population, and many remain unemployed.

Because they come from different countries, South Americans often have different reasons for migrating. Some move to North America to flee political instability and oppression. However, it seems that the faltering economies of the nations of South America have motivated most immigrants to move north. Popular tales of plentiful, high-paying jobs in North America still circulate among the young people of countries such as Ecuador, enticing thousands each year to leave home.

After World War II, many South American nations launched programs to modernize farming and in-

dustries, which eventually resulted in various economic and social problems, such as unemployment in over-crowded urban areas. Many farmers and other rural people, replaced by mechanization, moved to larger cities looking for work, but urban businesses did not expand fast enough to provide jobs for all of them. For example, in Colombia, the Cauca Valley project, which was initiated to control floods and generate electricity, attracted industry to the city of Cali. Many people from the surrounding countryside moved to the city to obtain industrial jobs in Cali and no longer looked to the land for their livelihood. The population of the city grew at an annual rate of eight percent during the late 1950s and early 1960s. Poor laborers migrating from the countryside accounted for most of the increase. The majority of the people who moved to Cali had no marketable job skills, and they worked as common laborers for less than a dollar a day.

In major cities throughout South America, internal migrations from rural to urban areas resulted in serious social tensions. The poor who moved to cities lived in shantytowns and often had no access to clean water, health care, or schools for their children. Those living in the countryside saw the inequity of their life when compared to the wealth of some city dwellers, who owned cars and homes, ate well, and could provide for their children. Today many South American cities are jammed with poor people who came to the cities to look for jobs but have not found them.

The migration of the rural poor within South America has influenced the pattern of emigration from the continent. Many South American immigrants now living in the United States and Canada have fled the crowded conditions and poor economies in their own countries. They tend to be richer than the poor who have crowded South American cities in recent decades. This is because the one-way airfare from Guayaquil, Ecuador, to New York City, for example, is at least $300,

In April 1948, a man walks through the Plaza Victorio in Bogotá, where burned-out buildings are evidence of the outbreak of political violence. "La Violencia," as the period of upheaval and revolt is known, gripped Colombia from 1948 to 1962.

an amount only within the reach of the middle and upper classes in South America. For many South Americans, migrating to the United States and Canada today is made easier because they have relatives or friends who are already living in North America.

Most Ecuadoran, Colombian, and Peruvian immigrants in the United States and Canada—both legal and illegal—were skilled workers in their home country. They were social workers, mechanics, barbers, or grocers. However, their standard of living in their homeland was well below that of the average U.S. worker. For example, they could not afford cars, washing machines, electric stoves, or vacations that lasted longer than a day or two at the beach. But unlike many of the millions of desperately poor who crowd South

America's cities, they were able to eat nutritious meals every night. Their houses were large enough to permit adults to sleep in rooms separate from their children. They were of a higher social class than many of the country's other urban residents.

Thousands of South American emigrants have been forced to give up their skilled positions and take jobs as floor sweepers and dishwashers when they arrive in the United States and Canada. For many, the sacrifice was worthwhile because political and economic turmoil

In 1985, a man points to three-year-old Argentine currency that was being sold in an antiques store. The Argentine government issued new bills when it revaluated its currency to keep pace with inflation, a problem that many South American countries faced during the 1980s.

made it impossible for them to maintain a middle-class standard of life in South America. In Colombia, the country with the largest number of people in the United States today, the number of emigrants grew sharply in the early 1950s at the beginning of "La Violencia," a period of political upheaval and revolt that lasted from 1948 to 1962. Not surprisingly, these emigrants were mostly members of the middle class. In 1967, the United States admitted 32,100 Colombians as nonimmigrants (mostly on student and tourist visas). By 1971, the number had grown to 59,000, and by 1976 to 101,500. Many of these people remained after their visas expired.

Thousands of Argentine immigrants also came to North America when Argentina's economy careened out of control in the 1970s. Argentine immigration to the United States reached its peak in 1976, the same year as a harsh campaign of political repression was initiated by the military. Economic factors, such as the clear decline in employment opportunities in Argentina, continued to be a problem. Real wages declined sharply after 1976, and in 1982 most Argentines' paychecks could buy less than they could 10 years earlier. Reduced employment in manufacturing, and later in construction, led to the loss of more than 300,000 jobs from 1976 to 1982. During the same period, public-sector employment also fell off markedly, especially in state-owned utilities. From 1977 to 1982, emigration continued to increase annually. In 1983, the flight of Argentines from their country peaked at about 75,000 annually; since then it has fallen off slightly.

In 1988, Peru's economy, which had been struggling since 1983, went into a tailspin. The gross domestic product fell by 8 percent and inflation topped 1,700 percent. Peruvian money had become so valueless that in cities such as Lima it would have taken a suitcase filled with bills to pay for a hotel room for a night. A fierce war continues to be fought between the country's armed forces and Communist guerrillas in the highlands. Government statistics show that 38,000 Peruvians left their country in 1986, 66,000 in 1987, and 120,000 in 1988.

South Americans migrate to a variety of destinations, but the United States and Canada are the destinations preferred by many who can afford the transportation costs. Today there are as many as 500,000 Peruvians living in Florida, New York, and California, most of whom have entered with tourist visas and then stayed in the United States after their visas had expired. Others come to the United States and Canada without any entry documents. Because tourist visas to the United States are increasingly difficult to obtain, some travel agencies are now charging $2,500 to smuggle immigrants through Mexico. "Every time there is a round of price increases, we get a new round of visa requests," a South American diplomat said. "Most people say they're going on vacation because they know it's hard to get immigrant visas, but they all want to leave here for good."

Seeking a New Home

Of course, the United States and Canada have not been the only places that South Americans go to live. Many people wishing to leave their country often pack their bags for another destination in Latin America because those countries seem less foreign than the United States. Many probably agree with the young Peruvian engineering student who told a *New York Times* reporter that he did not want to go to the United States "because Latinos are treated as second-class citizens there. I won't feel so foreign in a Latin American country." For example, many rural emigrants from Colombia go to other South American countries, particularly Venezuela, and in smaller numbers, Ecuador and Panama. There are about 300,000 Colombians living legally in Venezuela and 700,000 living there illegally.

A Chilean airliner flies over the Andes on its way from Santiago to Buenos Aires, Argentina, in the early 1950s. Throughout the 20th century, many South Americans have chosen to migrate to other South American countries because they believe that they will feel more at home in those countries than they would in North America.

Emigrants from Suriname, a former Dutch colony, and Guyana, a former British colony, often move to the Netherlands and England, respectively, because they can speak the language of the European countries and because those countries have immigration policies that are more liberal toward citizens of their former colonies than toward other immigrants. Many natives of French Guiana, which is a part of the French nation, emigrate to France for similar reasons.

The United States remains a choice to Colombians who can afford the costs of travel, and for that reason there are many highly trained professional and technical people among them. The same is true for Peruvians, who also frequently travel to Chile, Paraguay, and Argentina. For Argentina, a country that seems to be losing its most highly trained professionals, the United States has become the major destination of its emigrants since the 1970s. By 1980, 22 percent of the Argentines abroad resided in the United States; almost 39 percent resided in Brazil, Paraguay, Uruguay, Bolivia, and Chile altogether. Only 11 percent lived in a group of 8 Western European countries. Canada and Australia, two countries that seem to be emerging as new options for Argentines, together receive only about four percent of Argentine immigrants. The remaining 24 percent migrated elsewhere in the world.

Living Together but Separately

Because South Americans began arriving in North America in large numbers since the 1940s, the communities that they have formed are also new. The largest South American community in the United States is in Jackson Heights in the New York City borough of Queens. The Jackson Heights "colony" was founded at the end of World War I when a few hundred highly trained professionals settled there because of its proximity to Manhattan. Jackson Heights now accommodates a large number of Colombians and is known to some as Chapinero, the name of a middle-class suburb in Bogotá, Colombia's capital city. Since the community was established, emigrants from South America, the West Indies, and Puerto Rico have settled in the area. They are replacing other ethnic groups that earlier chose to settle in Jackson Heights: Italians who left the Lower East Side of Manhattan, the Irish who moved from Manhattan in the 1940s, and Jews from Europe who first settled in Queens and then later moved to the suburbs. The Hispanics who live in Chapinero have made their presence obvious—newsstands throughout Jackson Heights are stacked with papers from Bogotá, Buenos Aires, Santiago, and Guayaquil that have arrived in the city only about two days after

These houses are located on a typical street in Jackson Heights, New York. Many South Americans who have moved to the New York City metropolitan area have settled in Jackson Heights, which is in the borough of Queens.

they have been published. Catholic and Pentecostal churches (Christian congregations that emphasize revivalistic worship, baptism, and faith healing) and botánicas (shops that sell crucifixes and statues of the Blessed Virgin) are located through the area. Some botánicas also sell potions to curse an enemy or to revive a dying love affair.

South American communities can be found in some of the larger cities in Florida and California, and in Chicago, Illinois. Because many South Americans, like other immigrants before them, arrive with very little

money to begin their new way of life, they have often settled in communities that were earlier inhabited by Irish or Italian immigrants. Much of the time they settle with other Hispanics, such as Puerto Ricans, Cubans, and Dominicans. In the large communities, however, the South Americans have tended to settle into separate neighborhoods divided by nationality. In New York City, for instance, there is a Colombian section, an Ecuadoran section, and an Argentine section. Their communities are distinct, but they rely on one another for support of their traditional way of life. Even to the immigrants who do not live there, the urban communities can be very important because they provide places for them to maintain contact with their culture. In the city's restaurants and stores immigrants can hear news about their native lands and speak, as many of them do, about one day returning to their homeland. Many Colombians are ambivalent about being identified as Colombians because of the widespread conception of Colombians as drug dealers. Although the stereotyping of Colombians as drug dealers does have some basis in reality (one of the world's largest drug syndicates is based in Medellín, Colombia), the vast majority of Colombian immigrants are not drug dealers. Similar to other immigrant groups, such as the Italian Americans, who have been misperceived as members of the Mafia, Colombians suffer from the highly visible conduct of a few of their number. Many Colombians who can afford it choose to live outside the Hispanic community so that they can live more like other Americans. But places such as Chapinero remain a special place for them to congregate.

Because they speak Portuguese rather than Spanish, Brazilians have a cultural identity that is much different from other South Americans. Although Brazilians make up about half of the population of South America, relatively few have come to North America, and those who have immigrated do not settle in Hispanic communities as frequently as other South Americans.

During the 1960s, more than 2,300 Brazilian immigrants came to the United States each year, but the Brazilian government began imposing emigration restrictions during the 1970s, and the flow dropped to an average of about 1,500 per year.

Many of the Brazilians in the United States, like those from other South American immigrant groups, are part of an educated professional group. Large numbers arrive as students and stay on after marrying U.S. citizens. During the 1980s, they mostly lived in areas where large universities are located. Large concentrations of Brazilians remain in Yolo County, California, and Tippecanoe County, Indiana, presumably because they are associated with the University of California at Davis or with Purdue University. Numbers of Brazilian nationals have also settled near the state universities in Wisconsin, Iowa, and Kansas.

According to research conducted by University of Florida anthropologist Maxine L. Margolis, Brazilians began coming in increasing numbers to New York City, Boston, Newark, Miami, and Los Angeles during the late 1980s. She estimates that approximately 80,000 Brazilians flocked to New York City between 1987 and 1989. Although there is no distinct Brazilian residential neighborhood in the city, the majority of Brazilians live in Queens. Most Brazilians in New York City are well-educated and skilled people who have fled the faltering economic conditions in Brazil that made maintaining a middle-class life-style difficult.

Margolis has documented that despite the education and skill levels of the Brazilian immigrants in the New York City metropolitan area, most are employed in menial jobs. Males often work as shoe shiners, dishwashers, waiters, taxi drivers, and street vendors. Female occupations include housekeeping and babysitting. For example, an accountant from Rio de Janeiro waits tables in Manhattan, and a chemical engineer works as a limousine driver in Queens. The language barrier and racial prejudice that Brazilian immigrants face may account for their employment in unskilled positions. Margolis also reports that most Brazilian immigrants in New York City plan to remain in the city from 2 to 10 years, save money, and then return to Brazil to buy a house, a business, or land.

A NEW BEGINNING

Most South Americans currently living in North America are members of families that have migrated since the mid-1960s. Beginning in the early 1980s, the arrival of South American immigrants has coincided with two economic events: a severe downturn in the South American economy and an upswing in economic growth in the United States that began after 1983.

The growth of the U.S. economy in the late 1980s, however, has been in the technological and service industries—such as computers, advertising, and insurance—which employ technicians, clerks, and cashiers. Meanwhile, jobs in such areas as manufacturing and agriculture have disappeared or have been taken by workers born and educated in the United States. There is widespread concern that Hispanics in the United States, including South Americans, are relegated to accepting the less desirable opportunities that are available in the U.S. job market and that they are being locked into menial, dead-end work. The burden is especially heavy for darker-skinned Hispanics, who are sometimes stereotyped by employers as drug smugglers and gang members.

Because South Americans tend to be better educated than other Hispanics and because many come from cities, the transition to U.S. society and culture has been easier for them than for other Latin American immigrant groups. But even so, their initial experience in the United States has often been difficult. Almost all have taken a step down in their social class. Many skilled workers from South America have taken jobs in the United States that they would have scorned in their old country.

South Americans are still a relatively new immigrant group, so it is difficult to say whether or not they will be able to establish a middle-class niche for themselves in North American society. It is true that some South Americans live in the poorer neighborhoods of large cities, but to some extent their isolation is chosen rather than imposed on them by North Americans. Like other immigrant groups, South Americans have continued to treasure their language and culture after emigrating.

Geraldo Heredia, for instance, settled in Hartford, Connecticut, after leaving Peru in 1984. He continues to speak to his two children in Spanish so they will not forget it. His family also attends regular meetings of the Bolognese Club, one of six Peruvian-American clubs in Hartford, where they discuss Peruvian history. Heredia thinks it is important that his children know all about Peru for them to be decent, hardworking adults. "They are not like other people who forget their culture," he said. "They know what Peru is like, have a concept of what Peru is. We have returned to visit with them."

Similar to many other South Americans coming to the United States, Heredia was a professional in his homeland but was forced to take a step down economically and socially when he came to the United States.

He had been an engineering professor in his native city of Lima, but when he arrived in Connecticut, despite having studied English so meticulously in school, the language suddenly seemed very difficult. Eventually he was able to get a teaching job in an elementary school in Hartford but that proved too much of an adjustment. Heredia now manages parking lots. "There was a great world we were looking at but we couldn't communicate

Geraldo Heredia, an engineering professor who emigrated from Peru to the United States in 1984, advises one of the parking-lot employees whom he supervises in Hartford, Connecticut.

with that world," he said. "When I saw all this I said I'm leaving tomorrow—the language is driving me crazy."

Heredia still speaks of returning to Lima but says the war-torn atmosphere and collapsed economy in Peru discourage him from doing so. Moreover, his mother and his brother have lived in the United States since 1964. And the longer he remains in the United States, the less certain he is that he will be able to keep his children in touch with their old culture. "The children are adopting the new culture," he said, adding that they have become accustomed to the luxuries of North America. "They will reach the point when they say 'I don't want to return to Peru.' We take them there on vacation, but when we go they just want to ride around in taxis."

Most South Americans hold themselves apart from other Spanish-speaking groups, but they are somewhat similar to other Hispanic groups in the sense that they do not want to assimilate quickly into the ranks of other residents of the United States and Canada. For instance, even though Heredia's brothers grew up in the United States, they married Peruvian women whom they met in Connecticut. Although most South Americans say they admire North American technological progress and its work ethic, they initially hope to adapt to North American society as little as possible. Colombians, Chileans, and other South Americans think of themselves as having a distinctly different and perhaps superior worldview than Anglo-Saxons, whose influence has dominated North American culture. They feel that they have a higher appreciation for art and music, a better grasp of humanistic values, and a more well-rounded personality than North Americans, whom they tend to regard as materialistic and one-dimensional. The attitude is not anything new; in the 19th century, European writers who were popular in the Spanish world criticized Anglo-Saxons in England and North

America for the real or alleged ills of the Industrial Revolution. Materialism, irreligion, greed, philistinism, and the lack of aesthetic integrity were supposedly Anglo-Saxon qualities that differed from the profound virtues that were thought to inhabit the souls of the Germans, the Poles, the French, and the Spaniards.

Young Bolivian Americans ride on a float in a Bolivian parade in Jackson Heights, New York. Many South Americans proudly maintain their cultural heritage after they migrate to North America.

A newspaper stand on Roosevelt Avenue in Jackson Heights, New York, offers newspapers and magazines from South America. Many South American immigrants, particularly Colombians, have settled in Jackson Heights, and many businesses there serve the South American immigrant community.

This is perhaps one reason why many South Americans, when they come to North America, often speak of a real or fictitious return to their homeland. Many live in communities where they remain more interested in the affairs of South America than of the United States or Canada. In the New York City area—especially in Jackson Heights—it is possible to buy Colombian newspapers from 15 different provinces and the capital with only a lag of a day or two. The most popular Colombian magazines are also available, and every four years New York City newspapers routinely note that crowds of Colombians dutifully report to their consulate in Manhattan to vote in their country's presidential elections. Peruvians have also voted in their national elections from the United States, but in smaller numbers.

In Toronto, Canada, and its suburbs, there is another cluster of South American immigrants that is somewhat more dispersed than in the cities of the northeastern United States. They still tend to gather in clubs and around the parochial schools where they send their children. South Americans who can afford the airfare take a trip to their homeland every two or three years to renew their ties with loved ones and to reacquaint themselves with their culture. With the recent decline in airfares between such cities as Bogotá and New York, the trip is affordable to nearly everyone.

For this reason, the first generation of South American immigrants have often clung strongly to their values. They characterize life in the United States as being inhospitable and alien. They complain about the climate that seems to create tropiclike conditions in the summer and arctic freezes in the winter. They complain, too, about the apparent lack of moral values among youths in the United States and fear, among other things, that their children will become involved in the drug culture and exchange their Latin values for more "nihilistic" North American ways. In cities throughout the United States and Canada, South Americans have sent their children to Roman Catholic parochial schools, where they can mix with other Latin Americans.

The Roman Catholic Church

One important way that South Americans have sought to preserve their culture is through the Roman Catholic church, particularly by enrolling their children in its

parochial schools, often at great economic sacrifice. After the first great immigration of South Americans in the 1960s, the New York archdiocese established the Spanish Apostolate, sponsored by the diocese of Brooklyn-Queens. An energetic Venezuelan priest, the Rev-

South American schoolgirls skip rope outside Our Lady of Fatima School, a parochial school in Jackson Heights. South American immigrants often enroll their children in parochial schools as a way of ensuring that their culture will be preserved and that their children will receive the moral instruction that the parents feel the North American public schools do not provide.

erend René Valero, started the program that grew to employ more than 50 Spanish-speaking priests. The Spanish Apostolate remains today an important center of social life for South Americans in the New York City area. Some parishes try to attract new members from both Central and South America by celebrating the liturgy as it is performed in Latin America. And those South Americans who joined have lobbied for other changes, such as masses conducted fully in Spanish. These changes have been opposed by other Catholics, such as the Irish Americans, who typically prefer a more

Catholics in South Ozone Park, Queens, observe the Via Crucix (Way of the Cross), a procession that takes place on Good Friday. The procession, which commemorates the 14 events associated with Christ's suffering and death, integrates the traditions of various Hispanic parishioners, including Ecuadorans, Colombians, and Peruvians.

conservative service. They object to the use of guitars in the masses and complain about the passionate, more demonstrative style of praying and singing.

Outside the church, South Americans have also interacted with each other by joining different social and professional organizations where they can speak their native language and enjoy the camaraderie of others who have recently arrived in the United States. Today one can open telephone books in New York, Chicago, or

A group of Ecuadoran immigrants enjoy their leisure time at the Ecuadoran Social Club in Long Island City, New York. Like other immigrant groups, South Americans have established social clubs to provide themselves with a common meeting place and to help newcomers adjust to life in North America.

Two professional fútbol *(soccer) teams compete in Buenos Aires, Argentina. Fútbol, the favorite sport of many South Americans, is enjoyed in recreational clubs that have been founded by South American immigrants throughout the United States and Canada.*

Los Angeles and find nearly every country in South America represented by an association: the Argentine-American Association, the Chilean-American Association, or the Colombian-American Association. Also, there is a proliferation of recreational clubs that give immigrants the chance to sit back and enjoy soccer, their favorite native sport, as well as indigenous fare such as Inca Cola and *anticuchos* (skewered cow's heart) from Peru. Some immigrants have tried to organize political clubs, but few have stayed afloat. On the whole, most South Americans who maintain ties with an ethnic community remain more interested in South American politics than U.S. politics.

South American immigrants have brought the differences between their native countries to North America. For example, Venezuelans and Colombians have traditionally been competitive with one another in South America, and in North America their rivalry continues. Also, in Colombia it is unusual for people from higher social classes to associate with people from lower classes. Today, in cities such as New York, prosperous Colombians have established elite professional clubs that hold cocktail parties and plan group vacations. Colombians who do not belong to these elite associations bitterly complain about their exclusion from these groups and the lack of help that they extend to more recent arrivals to the United States from Colombia.

Racial Divisions in North America: The Costeños in Chicago

The costeño community in Chicago provides a good example of the complexity of the relations between South American immigrants in the United States. The costeños are people from the northern coastal region of Colombia; they tend to be darker skinned and are of mixed African, Indian, and Spanish descent. At home, they live apart from the Spanish (mostly white) Colombians, who live in the interior cities of Bogotá, Medellín, and Cali. Colombians of European descent enjoy most of the economic advantages in Colombia because they are white. Educated costeños in Colombia are still hindered by the sluggish rate of growth in the northern coastal region, so more than 4,000 costeños have immigrated to the United States and settled in Chicago.

The Colombians in Chicago have brought with them the same regional and racial cleavages that exist in Colombia. The costeños socialize with each other and with other Latin groups, such as the Cubans, but they seldom interact with white Colombians. Like many other South Americans, they are Roman Catholic, and they often send their children to parochial schools to teach them traditional values and basic Spanish. The costeños are like the other Colombians who have settled in New York City, because most of them are very well educated and middle-class. Many are hesitant to become naturalized citizens. Spouses will often split their citizenship status: Whereas one will become a U.S. citizen, the other remains a Colombian citizen so that the family will have the option of returning to Colombia. The costeños often hold themselves aloof from blacks and Puerto Ricans, who tend to have lower incomes.

The organizations that the costeños have founded in Chicago are professional and elitist. The two most important organizations are the Cartagena Medical Alumni Association—organized by costeño doctors in the late 1960s—and the Colombianos Unidos para Labor Activista (Colombians United for Labor Activism.) The purpose of the Cartagena Medical Alumni Association was at first to raise funds for the medical school in Cartagena, Colombia, where many of the costeño physicians graduated. But gradually the group grew to include all kinds of costeño professionals who wanted to help Colombian newcomers establish themselves in Chicago. Both groups sponsor guest lecturers, show movies, and arrange social activities. Although the Cartagena group tends to be dominated by costeños, some white Colombians attend its meetings but do not enroll as members. Colombianos Unidos has Colombian members from all backgrounds, including costeños. Colombians in Chicago use both organizations as a way to remain in touch with the issues of their homeland and to meet immigrants who have just arrived. But neither group was formed with the specific purpose of breaking down the barriers that Colombians have built up between one another.

SETTLING IN

The clusters of Hispanic communities around the United States and Canada play a central role in helping South Americans retain their ethnicity in their adopted country. Most South Americans, at least when they first arrive, try to recast their culture in their homes and communities so that they can feel comfortable and so that their children can grasp their heritage. Teaching their children some traditions is a way that South Americans seek to counteract the permissiveness in non-Latin culture that they feel has led to crime, drug abuse, and disrespect for elders.

Ethnic Enclaves

Because of their fears of the immensity of North American cities and of the alien culture in which few speak Spanish, many newly arrived South Americans have chosen to live in ethnic enclaves. There they can find parochial schools for their children and grocery-

A Jackson Heights bodega sells Spanish-language newspapers and other merchandise popular with its South American clientele.

store clerks who speak their language. Many remain in the enclaves for the first few years until they feel acclimated to the alien North American society.

Not far from the subway lines leading from Grand Central Station in New York City, one steps into a world where many South Americans gather. In places such as Queens, so many Hispanics have congregated that many streets, including once-staid Roosevelt Avenue in Jackson Heights, throb with the cheerful sounds of merengue or *cumbia*, musical styles popular in Latin America.

The small specialty shops, restaurants, and bodegas (grocery stores that are usually owned by industrious Argentine or Cuban families) are important to the immigrant community. In New York City, a study showed that these storekeepers worked an average of 110 hours a week and that their spouses and children usually serve as clerks and cashiers. The stores specialize in the native fare that South Americans and other Hispanics consider the heart of a satisfying meal: the yucca, Goya rice and beans, Bustelo coffee, and canned guavas and *naranjillas*. They also stock the special kitchen utensils their customers would have found in their native lands such as espresso coffee makers and wooden *tostoneras*, a utensil used for flattening sliced green plantains. By the door near the cash register are trays of baked coconut squares and sweet guava-filled cakes to tempt a departing customer.

The prices in these grocery stores are generally higher than in the large supermarkets, and the American goods often are of lower quality. But the stores provide a valuable service because their owners speak Spanish, and many South Americans with their

Patrons enjoy their meal at Calle Viejo in Jackson Heights, New York. The restaurant, which is owned and operated by Colombian Americans, features Colombian cuisine.

new, larger income in the United States are apparently eager to buy goods that did not exist, or existed only for the very rich, in their home country. According to a study conducted by a Spanish-language radio station in New York City, Hispanics spend about the average amount every week on food as other residents of the city, although their income tends to be lower. They tend to spend three times as much on cigarettes and four times as much on beer as other groups.

Restaurants offering native fare have also sprouted up around New York City, and to a lesser extent in cities around the United States and Canada. Some, such as El Inca in New York, began attracting a large Anglo-American clientele by offering standard North American dishes along with its chicken and rice and Inca soup. Others are more authentic and serve dishes such as Bolivian-style beef and plates of fried pork with hominy. On Saturday nights young South Americans crowd into the darkened rooms of some of these restaurants to hear native musicians. On Sundays, the restaurants serve more traditional family meals to immigrants who have come to the city from the suburbs for a taste of home.

In the Toronto area, there is no strongly defined neighborhood of South American immigrants such as the one in New York City. There South Americans live in a part of the city where there are also Italian and French vendors. The establishment of an enclave such as the one in Jackson Heights has been hindered by the fact that South Americans have moved there in fewer numbers. And in Canada many of the immigrants have found that it is cheaper to settle in suburbs such as Mississauga or Brampton than in Toronto itself. In the suburbs, South American families tend to meet by sending their children to the same Catholic parochial schools or settling in the same subdivisions dispersed through the area. For example, when Ursula Noriega, 18, flew from Lima, Peru, to Toronto with her family in 1988, they

(continued on page 81)

FAITH, FAMILY, AND COMMUNITY

Overleaf: *Elvia Quijano (left) meets with two other Colombian Americans outside Our Lady of Fatima, a Roman Catholic church in Jackson Heights, in New York City's borough of Queens. A large number of immigrants from South America, especially Colombians, have settled in the Jackson Heights section.*

South American immigrants are often members of middle-class families that have adapted to life in North America relatively quickly. The Xaubet family, who hail from Ecuador, go about their daily routine. Othello Xaubet (above), who is employed at United Press International, leaves for work from the family's home in Corona, New York. Marta Xaubet (upper right), Othello's spouse, teaches at P.S. 19, a school for partially disabled students. Their son Yves (lower right) plays the piano for his father. The younger Xaubet, who was born in the United States, studies classical piano at Hunter College in New York City.

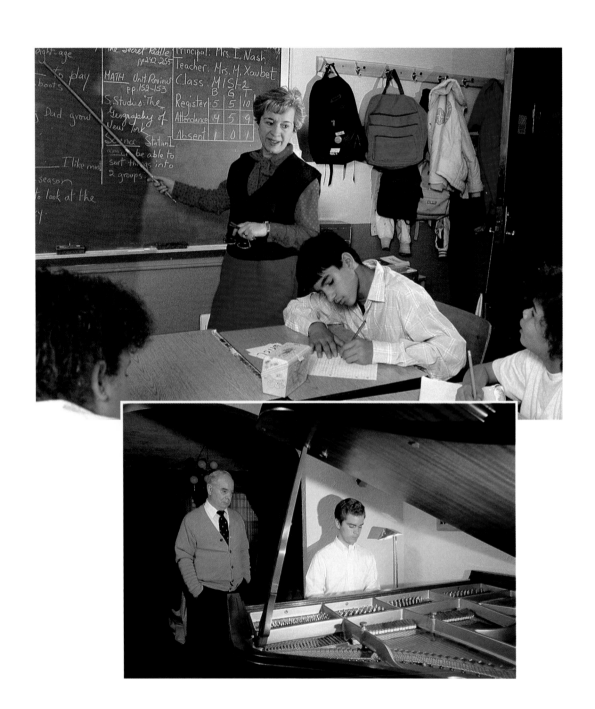

Many South Americans are skilled workers who make significant contributions to their adopted country. The members of the Quijano family, who live in Jackson Heights, are Colombian Americans. Elvia Quijano (upper left) works at All Nations Realty, a real estate agency in Jackson Heights. Hernando Quijano (lower left), an architect associated with Richard Dattner Architects in New York City, examines plans for a building. The Quijanos' U.S.-born son, Maurice (above), reviews the balance sheet of the restaurant that he owns and operates in New York City.

A sidewalk vendor offers mangoes in varying degrees of ripeness for sale along Roosevelt Avenue in Jackson Heights. South American immigrants can find foods popular in their homeland in stores throughout the community.

Parishioners worship at Our Lady of Fatima Church in Jackson Heights. Most South Americans are Roman Catholic, and Roman Catholic churches in North America have provided South American immigrant communities with many services, including educating their children in parochial schools.

South American youths play fútbol (soccer) in a playground in Jackson Heights. The children of South American immigrants, who are being reared and educated in North America, face a bright future with abundant opportunities in their parents' adopted country.

(continued from page 72)

had no relatives or friends in the area. But today she has met others from Ecuador, Peru, and Colombia in her parochial school in Mississauga.

Adjusting to a New Life

Adjusting to North American ways has been difficult for most South American immigrants, and that is why the South American enclaves in various cities, especially in the Northeast, have helped immigrants. For example, Rosa Tapias-Calpa, a Chilean who came to the United States because of political and economic instability, settled in the Hartford, Connecticut, area. A socialist, she said she was fired from her job as a quality-control inspector for a state-run medical laboratory in

Tahuantinsuyo, a band composed of musicians from Peru and Bolivia, plays traditional instruments in their performance of music native to the Andes.

Chile when a military coup toppled the popularly elected leftist government of Salvador Allende in 1973. She was unable to get another job while the military regime was in power, and she and her husband could not support themselves and their two children on his income alone.

Like many South Americans, Tapias-Calpa did not initially attempt to go to the United States. She and her husband first went to Argentina, where she worked as a housekeeper. In 1976, however, the military took over the government in Argentina and began to arrest and deport Chilean socialists. Fearing reprisal if she was forced to return to Chile, Tapias-Calpa was granted political asylum in the United States in 1977.

Eight months pregnant and unemployed, Tapias-Calpa stayed at home and worked as a baby-sitter for local Colombian families in Bridgeport, Connecticut, when she first arrived. In 1979, she and her husband opened a Chilean restaurant in Hartford and worked at it for a year and a half. There were few Chileans in Hartford, however, and the business catered mainly to Puerto Ricans in the area. The couple changed their menu to mostly Puerto Rican fare, keeping *empanadas* (meat pastries) as their only native course. They shut down the restaurant in 1981 when they divorced. She has since married a Colombian immigrant, Servio Calpa, who paints houses for a local contracting company.

In her first years in the United States, Tapias-Calpa said she often longed to return to Chile, where her parents still lived. But Tapias-Calpa's mother and father died while she was living in the United States. Now her oldest son has married a Colombian and is beginning a family in Florida. She would still like to raise her other two children in her native Chile, but she has developed roots in the United States.

When Tapias-Calpa came to the United States with her first husband, she assumed a new responsibility that many women from South America encounter when

they come north. She was forced to adopt a greater role in earning a living than women usually do in her native Chile. There the machismo and marianismo—the widely accepted notions in South America of how men and women should behave—force women into different roles than in the United States. In South America, men usually earn most of the income, and women normally stay at home to raise the children or work in unskilled positions. But in the United States, Tapias-Calpa was divorced from her husband in 1981; she had to find a way to support herself and her three children. For five

Rosa Tapias-Calpa, an immigrant from Chile, prepares a meal in her Hartford, Connecticut, home with the assistance of her two daughters.

months Tapias-Calpa was forced to live on welfare in a poor ghetto in Hartford. But friends she met when she and her husband ran their Chilean restaurant helped her get waitressing jobs, first at a Colombian restaurant and later at a Peruvian one. Soon she met more people while working who were able to help her get her next job, selling advertisements to Spanish-speaking merchants for a Hartford television station that broadcasts in several languages for various ethnic groups.

With the help of her friends and her new husband, Tapias-Calpa was able to find a comfortable home in a small town in Connecticut. But she still maintains her strong ties with other South Americans in the community and wants her children to do the same. She and her husband prefer to remain at home, but they faithfully attend parties thrown by other immigrants from Colombia or Chile in the area. As soon as she made enough money, Tapias-Calpa was able to send her children to a Catholic school rather than to public schools in Hartford. She could not accept the fact that the public schools allowed her daughters to kiss boys openly in public and wear tight pants rather than the skirts schoolgirls wear in Chile. Even when her oldest child had reached the age of 17, Tapias-Calpa forbade her daughters to go out on unchaperoned dates, to go to movies, or even to play records. She does not like to leave them alone in the house either, and when she goes to work during the summer when school is out, she often insists that the girls accompany her so that they can be watched. Tapias-Calpa remarks, "Many people say, 'How can you do this?'" But despite all her efforts, Tapias-Calpa said she believes her children are more like North Americans than Chileans. "I try to teach them my way, but everything they learn is American."

Living Separately

Not all of those settling in the United States and in Canada have decided to live in communities dominated by South Americans or even Hispanics. Orlando Cárdenas came to the United States in 1985 from Venezuela to live with his American wife, whom he met at the University of Venezuela. If he finds himself in any South American communities at all, he is a visitor. After earning a degree in agronomy (a field of agriculture dealing with soil management and improved crop production), Cárdenas moved to Oregon, where he worked as a supervisor in charge of shipping trees and plants to other nurseries around the United States. Later, he worked in fruit canneries in Oregon that made jellies and jams. With his employer, Cárdenas even invented a peach liquor that sells on the West Coast. In 1987 he moved to rural Connecticut and began working at a tree nursery. He supervised about 40 men and helped them with the daily chores of planting, pruning, trimming, and grafting trees. The company employed many Hispanics, mostly Puerto Ricans, and it needed a supervisor who could speak both Spanish and English.

Cárdenas said the most difficult thing for him to cope with in the United States has been the racial barriers. At work he has felt unable to make suggestions to his bosses because he is stereotyped as a poorly educated Hispanic. He remarked, "They are not used to Hispanics being in a position where they have a say about something. Sometimes it seems like they don't think you could know anything." But he thinks that he sees the reason for this: He feels that some Hispanics in the United States are not interested in bettering themselves and do not bother to attend college or even to learn English.

Cárdenas now has five children and said he would like them to know both Spanish and English and remain aware of their Venezuelan heritage. But he has no plans to return to Venezuela or to move to another community where they will live near other South Americans. When he first came to the United States, it was difficult to get a job because his English was poor. But he took classes at a state university, and he hopes to move up in the agronomy business by studying new methods of grow-

A group of Sendero Luminoso (Shining Path) guerrillas meet at a hideout in the Andes. The Sendero Luminoso, a band of approximately 2,000 fighters engaged in assassinating government officials and other "enemies of the revolution," seeks to establish an agrarian Communist society in Peru. The group has been responsible for more than 10,000 deaths since 1980.

ing trees and plants in his spare time. Cárdenas said he is grateful to the United States for giving him a chance to work hard and be prosperous: "I miss everybody [in Venezuela], but you have to look at the country and compare. You can have a better education here and live better if you work hard." His rural home in Eastford, Connecticut, has been a convenient place for him to live. He feels that he can save money and work hard enough to to achieve a higher standard of living than was possible in Venezuela.

Some South American immigrants face less difficulties in adjusting to life in the United States and Canada. Rising political violence since World War II and kidnappings in some South American countries have also caused the flight of some Europeans, Americans, and Jews who were citizens of South American countries. They have left because they became the target of rising violence directed against high-profile businessmen. For example, Noel Quenet grew up in Lima, Peru, where his British father worked as an executive of an American company in Lima. After serving in the Royal Air Force in World War II, he returned to Lima, where his mother lived, and he planned to spend the rest of his life there. Eventually, he rose to the position of general manager of the Peruvian-owned company that made Crystal beer, the most popular beer in Peru at the time. He remained in Lima after he retired in 1975, but with the growing strength of the Sendero Luminoso (Shining Path) Communist movement, whose avowed aim is a revolutionary overthrow of the Peruvian government, he said he may never return permanently. In 1989, he and his wife began spending most of their time in their homes in Nova Scotia and Florida. Although he maintained his Peruvian citizenship, Quenet no longer considers himself a Peruvian.

"Whether we go back now, I don't know," he said. "When people you know have been kidnapped and killed, you just don't know whether it's worth staying. You have to question yourself no matter how much you like it there." Quenet is barely aware of a South American community in the United States or Canada. He grew up speaking English and Spanish, so adapting to life in North America has been a minor adjustment for him.

Chilean-American women who are members of the International Ladies' Garment Workers' Union march in a Labor Day parade in Queens, New York. South American immigrants have made significant contributions to North American society.

MAKING
THEIR MARK

Most South Americans who have immigrated to North America have never known hunger at home; their motives for coming were more complex. Almost all of them come from cities and have specialized job skills. Many have made significant contributions to their adopted country in a variety of areas, including business, the performing arts, science, literature, and medicine. Many South Americans have succeeded in academic professions or in the field of architecture—a discipline held in high prestige in South America. Many who have come to be educated in the United States and Canada have stayed because they developed professional ties to the north or because they have been alienated by the politics of their home country.

One prominent architect and scholar who came to the United States from South America is Cesar Pelli, an immensely successful designer and former dean of the School of Architecture at Yale University. Born in

The Vienna International Center, which serves as the home of many United Nations agencies, was designed by Cesar Pelli, an Argentine-American architect. Several South Americans who have migrated to North America have achieved acclaim in the field of architecture, a discipline that is held in high regard throughout South America.

Tucumán, Argentina, in 1922, Pelli came to the United States in 1952 to study at the University of Illinois, Champaign-Urbana. He worked as a director of design for the Argentine government before immigrating to the United States, and after earning his master's degree from the University of Illinois, he began work as an associate for an architectural firm with offices in Michigan and Connecticut. He rose to prominence quickly and moved to Los Angeles to work as a director of design in an architectural firm from 1964 to 1968 and as a partner in charge of design in another from 1968 to 1977. During the 1960s, Pelli distinguished himself with innovative design methods for buildings, such as a circulation spine that replaced stairwells, lobbies, and lounges as places for people to meet. His most dramatic use of the circulation spine along the perimeter of buildings was his award-winning design for the UN building in Vienna, Austria, a multilayered space stretching the entire length of seven attached towers. He also distinguished himself for his design of the U.S. embassy building in Tokyo, Japan, which he cut off at many points to consciously avoid the large, monumental buildings designed by architects before him.

"My commitment is to architecture that celebrates life," he wrote for a book entitled *Contemporary Architects*, published in 1987. "For too long architects have been absorbed with death-defying qualities. An architect that defies death has to accentuate the qualities of the non-living. It seeks above all massiveness and durability and it avoids the temporary and the fragile. An architecture that enhances life accents perception, lightness and change."

After leaving Los Angeles in 1977 to become dean of the architecture school at Yale University, Pelli opened his own office and experimented with light building materials that blended with the cityscape around it. In 1977, he began working on a tower to expand the Museum of Modern Art in New York City, which he eventually designed to be sheathed in brown and gray glass to complement the brownstones of the streets in the area. He also designed the World Financial Towers in Manhattan, near the World Trade Center. He designed the towers to harmonize with the surrounding area by giving them the same proportions as the towers at the World Trade Center and by scaling the rooftops at the same height as other buildings in the area.

Another successful architectural scholar in the United States is Humberto Rodriguez-Camilloni, who has taught architecture and art at the college level since the early 1970s. Born in Lima, Peru, Rodriguez-Camilloni came to the United States in 1963 to study architecture at Yale University. He was awarded his bachelor's degree, magna cum laude in 1967, his master's degrees in architecture and philosophy in 1971 and 1973, and his Ph.D. in 1981. He returned to Lima for a short time to teach, but he felt alienated by the climate at the state university there, which is highly politicized and riddled with strikes and demonstrations. Returning to the United States, he taught as an assistant professor in the School of Architecture at Tulane University in Louisiana from 1975 to 1982. He moved to Virginia to teach in 1983, where he lives today.

When he came to the United States, Rodriguez-Camilloni said in an interview with the author in 1989, he had intended to stay only for a few years and to return to his native Lima to be near his family and teach in the universities there. "But man proposes and God disposes, you might say," he said. While at Yale he met the woman he would marry in 1972, and today they have two children. Today Rodriguez-Camilloni teaches at Virginia Polytechnic Institute and State University in Blacksburg, Virginia, where he also conducts research on the history of Latin American architecture, especially of the colonial period. He also travels to Peru and Argentina to work on restoration projects for the Organization of American States, which is based in Washington, D.C.

Because South Americans have come in large numbers to North America and Canada relatively recently, there are few obvious examples of descendants of South American immigrants who have risen to national prominence. Some people of South American ancestry are not recognized as part of the South American community in North America because they have anglicized their last names or have married North Americans.

For instance, Juan Trippe, U.S. air pioneer and former head of Pan American World Airways (Pan Am), had ties to South America. Although Trippe's ancestors migrated from England to Maryland in 1698, he was named Juan in memory of Juanita Terry, the Venezuelan wife of his great-uncle, whose family had helped colonize South America. Trippe, who was born in New Jersey in 1899 and was the son of an executive in the investment and brokerage business in New York City, spent most of his career in elite schools and business circles.

Trippe was educated in private schools in New York and Pennsylvania and from an early age was interested in flying. When he was 10 years old, he built model planes powered by elastic bands and flew them in Central Park. He was admitted to Yale in 1917 and took private flying lessons, with the result that he was admitted into the fledgling Naval Flying Service. He left

Passengers prepare to board a Pan American World Airways airplane in the late 1920s. The airline, which grew into the world's largest, was founded in 1927 by Juan Trippe, whose great-aunt was Venezuelan.

college hoping to fight in World War I but returned to Yale when the armistice was signed in 1918.

After graduating in 1921, he became a bond salesman with the banking firm of Lee, Higginson, and Company. He intended to join the family brokerage firm, Trippe and Company. But in early 1923, he read in a trade publication that the navy was offering 9 surplus planes for sale, and with former members of the Yale Flying Club, he bought 7 of them for $500. With the planes, Trippe organized Long Island Airways, Inc., at Rockaway Beach, New York, where passengers were picked up for sightseeing tours. Charter services were also furnished, and the company performed occasional work for motion pictures as well. In 1924, he persuaded a group of Boston bankers to lend him the money to establish the Colonial Transport Company, which started the first airmail delivery on a contractual basis.

In 1927, Trippe and two wealthy, aviation-minded friends created Pan Am by bidding for the first international airmail-carrying contract. He supervised the company as it grew to be the world's largest commercial airline, with extensive lines running around the South American continent.

Another successful person born in a South American country was Edwin Lefevre, a writer and journalist in the early 20th century. Lefevre was born in Colón, Colombia, a region that became part of the Panama Canal Zone after Panamanian rebels, with U.S. encouragement, successfully revolted and declared independence from Colombia. Lefevre's father, a citizen of the United States, married a Colombian woman while working in Panama as an agent of the Pacific Mail Steamship Company. After Panama's declaration of independence, Edwin Lefevre's maternal grandfather became a chief justice in the Panamanian Supreme Court, and his great-uncle became president of Panama. Edwin, however, decided to remain in the United States after going to college, and he started working as a reporter for the *New York Sun* in 1890 and became financial editor of *Harper's* magazine. Through the 1920s he became regarded as an authority on Wall Street activities and conditions and wrote several books based on his experiences as a reporter.

Most South American immigrants are accustomed to more modest successes than Juan Trippe, who grew up speaking English and enjoying substantial family support. Many South Americans have been preoccupied by the problems of adjusting to the New World, and the more prominent ones among them are those who help others adjust to the alien climate.

Juan Brito, a social worker employed by the Hartford public schools, is one South American immigrant who has become well known in the Northeast for the assistance that he has given to needy families. Born in Chile in 1948, Brito came to the United States in 1973 after losing his job when the government of Salvador Allende was overthrown. He arrived as a student, seeking a degree in social work. His wide range of extracurricular activities included working as a community organizer in Hartford neighborhood centers and as a social worker at a local elementary school, editing the Spanish-language newspaper *¿Qué Pasa?*, organizing a cultural evening where Latin American music was performed, and serving on the boards of several cultural and civic organizations.

As a social worker, Brito works primarily with Hispanic students who have emotional problems—those who show signs of depression; those who are going through a crisis, such as the death of a parent; those who are the victims of child abuse; and those who are chronically absent or late at school. He goes to the home of some to talk with their parents.

Even after 13 years in the United States, Brito said his loyalties are still divided. He socializes with Puerto Ricans in the city, and in 1977 he married a Puerto Rican woman who is a bilingual teacher in one of the elementary schools. But similar to many other Chileans who have come to the United States, he is politically conscious of events in his native country. In 1988, he was part of a delegation from the American Federation of Teachers that observed a Chilean plebiscite in which voters ended the 14-year rule of dictator General Augusto Pinochet. Brito still considers returning to his hometown of Santiago, Chile, where he would like to start a community newspaper.

"That's the problem with exile," he told the Hartford *Courant* in 1989. "When you make the decision to leave the country, really you are doing a lot of things with your life that are difficult to change. You marry, you have relationships with the city. I belong to some boards in the area. I feel responsible for the Hispanic population in many aspects. It isn't easy to say goodbye after 16 years and go back there."

TOWARD A BRIGHTER FUTURE

Perhaps the most important issue concerning South American immigrants is how quickly they will learn English, become naturalized citizens of the United States or Canada, and grow more involved in North American politics rather than in the politics of their homeland. Many South Americans who come to North America cling to their own language and cultural traditions longer than immigrants from other countries. Unlike such groups as the Polish and Chinese Americans, South Americans have found it easy to visit their native country for a short time, renew their cultural ties, and return to the United States or Canada to make more money. In fact, many come to North America planning to work for a few years, save some money, and then return to their native country permanently.

During the late 19th century and early 20th century, large waves of European immigrants in the United States filtered through the public school systems in large cities such as New York, Philadelphia, Chicago, and Cleveland. Classes were conducted only in English in these schools. Immigrant families often forbade their children to use their Old World languages at home because they wanted their children to become Americans as quickly as possible.

South Americans have encountered a different experience than most European immigrants because affordable airline travel has made it easier for them to visit their native land after they have emigrated. Also, most South Americans arrived in the United States during or after the civil rights movement, in which blacks established a national recognition of the rights and needs of ethnic minorities. Operating in this liberal climate, many Hispanics, including South Americans, successfully lobbied for bilingualism in some public school systems. Therefore, South Americans have greater choices when it comes to deciding whether to learn English or to continue using their native language by remaining in communities where the schools offer bilingual education.

Nevertheless, South Americans have tended to learn English and to adapt to living in North America more quickly than other Hispanics, primarily because most South American immigrants come from middle-class homes, arrive with technical skills, and appreciate the rewards of education. They recognize the need to learn English to obtain higher-paying jobs in North America. That may change, however, and so the future of the South American community in the United States and Canada depends to a great extent on whether political and economic problems force more of them to come north.

One of the main arguments among journalists, academics, and politicians is over the extent to which the United States is responsible for the economic and political calamities in South America. Critics of the United States, for instance, often say that repression in South America is fostered by U.S. military aid to right-

Two men check over the airfares posted in the window of a travel agency in Brooklyn, New York, that caters to immigrants from Latin America. Modern airline travel has enabled South American immigrants to renew their ties with their culture easily and relatively inexpensively.

wing regimes; some of the South American officers who have led the coups were trained at the School of the Americans in the Panama Canal Zone and in Fort Benning, Georgia. Defenders of U.S. foreign policy and some South Americans insist that the problems faced by the nations of South America have more to do more with the historical and socioeconomic circumstances of the continent.

North Americans are certain to become more bound
to South America in the future as the United States and
Canada become increasingly attractive as beacons of
personal liberty and economic opportunity for the

Two immigrants fill out an application for legal residency in the United States under the amnesty provisions of IRCA. South American immigrants are part of the growing Hispanicization of North America, a trend that is likely to create many important social issues in the years to come.

peoples of the Western Hemisphere. South Americans who have already immigrated to North America have shown they can adapt quickly to a new life. That may change if political turmoil and economic decline in

South America persists, prompting poorer South Americans who are desperate for work and willing to enter the United States and Canada illegally to move north in large numbers. Poorer, less educated immigrants may pose more problems, such as unemployment, for their adopted country because they do not possess the same degree of ability as those South Americans who have already immigrated to North America.

Illegal immigration has become a major problem for the United States. Under U.S. law, 290,000 aliens, with a maximum of 20,000 from each foreign nation, are allowed to enter the country annually for the purpose of immigration. Because only a small number of people are granted immigration visas each year, many prospective immigrants must wait for years before they can legally immigrate to the United States. As a result, more than 1 million aliens enter the country illegally each year.

In 1986, Congress passed the Immigration Reform and Control Act (IRCA) in an attempt to curb the flow of illegal aliens into the country. IRCA provided a onetime amnesty for millions of people, including South Americans, who were already economically integrated into American society. The act also established stiff penalties, such as large fines and prison terms, for employers who hire undocumented aliens. IRCA requires employers to ask all new employees to provide documentation that they are U.S. citizens or aliens eligible to work in the United States. By penalizing employers who hire illegal aliens, Congress hoped that there would be less incentive for people to enter or remain in the United States illegally. However, a number of Hispanics who are U.S. citizens or legal immigrants have found that some employers, despite laws forbidding discrimination on the basis of race or national origin, are reluctant to hire them because they fear that anyone of Hispanic appearance may be an illegal immigrant.

The Future for South American Immigrants

Like many immigrant groups today, South Americans are at a crossroads in the United States. It is difficult to say whether they will be able to achieve the middle-class life-style that they were accustomed to in their native country. Although many South Americans and their descendants have become assimilated into North American culture, others cling to their various traditions and speak of one day returning to their homeland. Many come to North America for the economic advantages that it offers but remain critical of it as a society that is fraught with problems of materialism, drugs, and crime. It remains to be seen whether the sons and daughters of these immigrants will move away from their communities in large cities and lose touch with the traditions that their parents brought with them. Some may decide to join communities with Hispanics of other nations, whose language is often the same but whose traditions are somewhat different, to preserve as much of their cultural heritage as possible.

Despite all the hardships of life in North America, thousands of South Americans consider the adjustment to life in the United States and Canada well worth the effort. North America provides the immigrants with greater opportunities than they had at home, even if they must start at the lower rungs of the economic ladder. It seems likely that the children of South Americans, who are being reared and educated in North America, will be able to attain a high standard of life. Even though South Americans are a relatively new and small immigrant group in North America, they have added diversity to the culture mosaic. Indeed, the presence of South Americans is part of the significant surge in North America's Hispanic population. The "Hispanicization" of the United States in particular has been one of the most significant demographic trends of the last 20 years and is expected by many to become increasingly important in the years to come.

FURTHER READING

Gann, L. H., and Peter J. Duignan. *The Hispanics in the United States: A History*. Boulder, CO: Westview Press, 1986.

Kessner, Thomas, and Betty Boyd Caroli. *Today's Immigrants: Their Stories*. New York: Oxford University Press, 1982.

Margolis, Maxine L. "Brazilians in the Big Apple." *The Brazilians* 193 (February/March 1990): 4–5.

Marshall, Adriana. "Emigration of Argentines to the United States." In *When Borders Don't Divide*, edited by Patricia R. Pessar. New York: Center for Migration Studies, 1988.

Ramirez, Manuel III. "Cognitive Styles and Cultural Democracy in Action." In *Toward Multiculturalism: A Reader in Multicultural Education*, edited by J. Wurzel. Yarmouth, ME: Intercultural Press, 1988.

Reimers, David M. *Still the Golden Door*. New York: Columbia University Press, 1985.

Skidmore, Thomas E., and Peter H. Smith. *Modern Latin America*. New York: Oxford University Press, 1984.

Thernstrom, Stephen, et al., eds. *The Harvard Encyclopedia of American Ethnic Groups*. Cambridge: Harvard University Press, 1980.

Weyr, Thomas. *Hispanic U.S.A.: Assimilation or Separatism?* New York: Harper & Row, 1988.

INDEX

PICTURE CREDITS

ALAN CULLISON, whose mother was born in Lima, Peru, is a reporter for the Hartford *Courant*, covering courts and prisons. He received a B.A. in American history from the University of Chicago, where he concentrated his studies on the history of ethnicity in U.S. politics. He was born in New York City and now lives in Hartford, Connecticut.

DANIEL PATRICK MOYNIHAN is the senior United States senator from New York. He is also the only person in American history to serve in the cabinets or subcabinets of four successive presidents—Kennedy, Johnson, Nixon, and Ford. Formerly a professor of government at Harvard University, he has written and edited many books, including *Beyond the Melting Pot, Ethnicity: Theory and Experience* (both with Nathan Glazer), *Loyalties*, and *Family and Nation*.